# The
# Just
# Before Bed
# Journal

30 Days of Tips and Prompts to Get
Your Life on Track and Keep It There

*Created By*
## David Soto Jr.

ISBN: 9781696200349

# Introduction

If you are reading this, I want to congratulate you on being someone who is about to take action. What I have laid out for you in this book can be life-changing.

If you are still in a bookstore and haven't made the purchase yet, let me fill you in on a little secret before you buy: What's in this journal I did for years in a simple spiral note pad. You can get a nice one at Target for about $2.95. Find yourself a pencil, and you'll be on your way to making some serious changes in your life on the cheap.

I did this off and on for years. The problem is, I like structure. I like the numbers being there for me. I like the blank lines. I like having a place for the date. And, more than anything, I like to be efficient.

Every day before I wrote in my spiral notepad, I had to write the words: Accomplishments, Gratitude, and Tomorrow. Yeah, this isn't much, but I always thought it would be easier to have the headings already there. I wanted the ease of just opening the journal and writing down my five things under each heading.

I recently bought a journal that I thought would be the solution to my problem. It was a little different—not exactly what I had been doing all these years—but I thought I would give it a shot. Ultimately, I gave up on it. I didn't like it.

A big reason I gave up on it was that it was nearly impossible to write on the left side of the book. I looked forward to every other day when I could write in it with ease. Also, there wasn't any space for Accomplishments and Tomorrow's To-dos, both of which I have found over the years to be very helpful to annotate.

Eventually, I thought, "I could do a better job than this." So I did.

Do I want to sell a million of these journals? Sure. Why not? But I will tell you that the reason I created this is for me. I will be the first person to buy it, and I promise that by the time you read these words, I will have a stack of brand new copies in my home waiting for me to use.

## How does it work?

Keep the journal someplace handy—where you are every night before bed. It might be your nightstand, or it might be on your coffee table in front of the TV. The point is to have it somewhere where you will be able to write in it every night.

Write down twenty things. Five of each of the following: personal accomplishments, things you are grateful for, affirmations, and to-dos for tomorrow. That's it. The whole process could take just a couple of minutes, but you'll be surprised how often you'll sit there for a long time trying to think of one more thing to be grateful for or whether something you did is worth writing down as an accomplishment or not. Hint: It is.

# Gratitude

"The more you are grateful for what you have, the more you will have to be grateful for." ~Zig Ziglar

Here are just some areas in life you can expect to improve upon when you start to express gratitude daily:

- Relationships
- Physical health
- Mental health
- Stress reduction
- Sleep
- Self-esteem

Is there anyone who *doesn't* want improvement in any of these?

I am not just making this up. There are studies out there that back up everything listed above. I could include them in this text but let's face it studies are kind of boring. Also, there is always at least one that will support any opinion out there. Because of this, I prefer to take a common-sense look at it.

Can you name a negative effect of being grateful? Can you name a person who had or a moment in history where there was too much gratitude? Has anyone ever genuinely thanked you for something you did and it resulted in anger, fear, or resentment? Can you even imagine a scenario where there is too much gratitude in a situation? I'm betting not. I'm willing to say that there is not one negative thing that can result from giving thanks.

## How does receiving gratitude feel?

When someone thanks you for something you did—an act of service, a display of your creativity, or just doing something you'd consider a normal everyday task—how does that make you feel? You may blow it off and say something like, "just doing my job," or "it's no problem." But the truth is, it feels good to be appreciated. It's the number one thing employees want. Not more money, not better benefits, not longer paid vacations. They want to feel appreciated.

Remember that feeling of appreciation and know that this is the energy you are putting out in the world when you show some gratitude. And if you are putting it out there, that means it's going to come back.

## It's not a secret

Now, do you know about the law of attraction? Putting that energy out there brings it back to you, some say tenfold.

If you have ever taken the time daily to express gratitude, like for example in a journal (wink wink), you may have noticed good things happening to you.

Since I started journaling years ago, I've noticed that when things are not going my way, it's also when I have stopped writing down five things that I am grateful for every day. When I pick it back up, the good things start happening again.

## No room for hate

The one thing that I feel gratitude does is drive out hate. If there is gratitude in your heart, there is no room for hate. Why is this? Because the opposite of hate IS gratitude. You may think that it's love but have you ever loved something and feel hate for it at the same time. You have surely heard of the term "a love-hate relationship." Gratitude and hatred are on the same emotional spectrum. Think of it as a sliding scale. The more appreciation you have for something in your life, the less you can hate it.

Do I even need to ask you to name a negative effect of being hateful?

## How do you do it?

In this journal, you will write down five things you are grateful for every night just before bed. The best part about this exercise is that if you haven't been thankful for anything yet that day, you will be just before bed. When I first started doing this, I loved how the process forced me to be grateful. If I didn't have to write down five things I was thankful for, I wouldn't have expressed gratitude at all that day.

It doesn't have to be deep either. It could be as simple as the roof over your head, the food you eat or having hot water to shower. There are people out there in the world who don't have these things. When you think about this, it makes it very easy to be grateful.

Sometimes I expressed gratitude for things I didn't have or wasn't really thankful for. I gave thanks many a night for my income and "hassle-free" rental properties. The truth was, I wanted more income and wanted my rental properties to be hassle-free. They weren't.

What I was doing, in this case, was creating the world I wanted. I used the gratitude section of my journal to write down a couple of affirmations. This is why the journal you are holding in your hands now has a place specifically for that but more on affirmations later.

# Accomplishments

"Look for small victories and build on that. Each small victory…gives you confidence. You realize that these little victories make you feel great, and you keep going."
~Arnold Schwarzenegger

Positive reinforcement is the key to successful training. Whether the trainees are students, dogs, offspring, or employees; the best way to teach them to do something is to reward the behavior you want. (BTW, this is for mammals in general, so unless your kid is a fish, positive reinforcement will always work.)

## Attaboys and Attagirls

We love them. We love getting praised for something we have done. We love it so much that we'll instinctually do something again to get another one. This is why, as the parent, boss, or teacher, we have to be careful about what we reward.

Behavior that is rewarded will be repeated. Reinforce the dog's barking or the child's temper tantrum, and it will happen again, guaranteed.

Basically, pats on the back feel good and we'll do anything we can to get more but why wait for someone else to give them to us. Why not give ourselves pats on the back and attaboys?

Give yourself credit for some of your accomplishments every night before you go to bed. They could be minor, or they could be huge. What I have learned over the years is that whether I write down something as miniscule as "wrote 500 words" (my daily goal is 1000) or as major as "launched a new book," either feels pretty dang good to acknowledge.

Stop being so hard on yourself and give yourself the credit you deserve.

## How do you do it?

Write down five accomplishments, no matter how small. If you have problems thinking of any, then this is precisely why you need this daily exercise. Do not leave any of these lines blank.

# To-do

"Plan your day the night before." ~Jack Canfield

My second job outside of the Air Force gave me the title of Maintenance Supervisor. For a young man of 24, it was the most responsibility I ever had. I quickly learned that if I wanted to be any good at it, I was going to have to get organized. One of the keys to making my first position as a supervisor a success was a checklist.

Before I went home every day, I made a checklist for the morning and left it on my desk. This list was how I knew what to do as soon as I got in the next day. But there was an added benefit.

In doing this daily, I noticed that when I left the job, I didn't have to think about work until the next day. I wasn't going to forget to do anything either because I had written everything down. Work did not weigh heavily on my mind when I was off, and this allowed me to relax or pursue other activities.

Later in life, during times where I didn't have to work, it occurred to me that I could continue this practice. Why not make a personal "to-do" list for the next day? Get a haircut, write 1000 words, send a message to (anyone), do laundry, go to the bookstore.

I eventually put this into play around 2014, when I started journaling nightly. I don't have a precise example of the impact it had on my life, but as I said in the introduction, things seem to go well when I journal on a nightly basis. Since the beginning, I have always included writing down five things to do tomorrow.

## It allows you to relax

Just like writing a to-do list before I left work, I find that writing a personal to-do list before bed enables me to forget about what I have to do tomorrow and relax. I think of it as a download—getting all those things off your mind for the night.

This will come in very handy for those of you who are worrywarts and have trouble falling asleep because you are thinking of all the stuff you have to do the next day.

## You have all night to work on a solution

According to Jack Canfield, when you write down your tough tasks in the evening, you are giving your subconscious all night long to work on them. Without having to think (or worry) about it, you may wake up with a solution to whatever problem you have to face that day.

## It helps you remember what you have to do the next day

One thing that I can attest to with this practice is that writing things down helps me remember them. And if I do happen to forget something, I'll be reminded of it the next night when I open up my journal.

## You'll fall asleep faster

This may have something to do with the first item on this list, but when I went to do a little research for this topic, all of my page-one results were of a study released in January of 2018. This study concluded that people who wrote down what they needed to do the next day fell asleep nine minutes faster than the people who wrote down their accomplishments for the day. Luckily we do both in this journal.

One of the most gratifying things I find every night when I open my journal is being able to cross off the things on my previous night's to-do list. Drawing a line with my pencil through the to-dos I wrote down the night before is one of the most gratifying things I have ever experienced.

## How do you do it?

Write down five things that you have to do tomorrow. They could be personal like, "Get groceries" or they could be work related like, "Submit TPS reports."

# Affirmations

"The key to success is to focus our conscious mind on things we desire not things we fear." ~Brian Tracy

For most people, affirmations are some kooky, weird mumbo-jumbo. I used to be one of these people, but I must have gotten so low in my life that I was willing to try anything. One day, I started reading aloud the affirmation card that came with Zig Ziglar's motivational tapes. It was long, tedious, and not fun, but I persisted—for a while.

After about a month or so, I hadn't become rich, didn't have an incredible career, my dream home, or the girl of my dreams. My life still sucked, and like most things I tried, if it didn't get results right away, I gave up on it. What I didn't give up on was the use of a planner Zig always mentioned in his talks.

It was a hardbound daily planner where you could write down your daily activities. For years, I wrote down everything I did, every minute of the day. I'm not sure what the benefit was but it was also a goal planner. In the back you would write out your personal and professional goals, keeping them handy so you could review them whenever you wanted.

I learned to write these goals down in the first person present tense. So instead of writing down something like, "publish a photo," I would write down, "I am a published photographer."

At the top of each page of the planner, above your daily activities, was a space for you to write down your weekly goals. Here you would pick a couple of your big goals from the back and a couple of smaller ones. You would write them all down on the far left and then every day that week you'd jot down a note of how you worked towards it that day. When I wrote my weekly goals down here, I also wrote them down in the first person present tense.

I did this for quite a few years. I may have achieved some goals but I never became rich. That seemed to be the most important thing in my life at the time. So after years of using this planner and the goal of being rich never came to fruition, I gave it up.

Several years must have passed when I stumbled across a plastic tote full of these very planners. As I thumbed through them, I couldn't believe what I was reading. Nearly everything I had written down so many years prior had come true.

This opened my eyes. I realized the power of writing down the things I wanted in life, so I took up the practice again. This time, not bothering with buying a planner and writing down everything I did every minute of the day but rather just writing down my goals in first person present tense—affirmations. I picked up a lined journal and divided my goals into categories: professional, financial, social, health, creative. If I could imagine it, I wrote it down.

- I am debt-free.
- I am a published photographer.
- I have a 36" waistline.
- I speak Spanish.
- I am a published author.
- I own rental properties.
- I travel for months at a time.
- I am a father.

- I live near a body of water. (Let me tell you about this one.)

All of these came true—none of them overnight. For example, it took me years of classes and traveling to learn Spanish. I'm not fluent (yet), but I can hold a conversation, do some translating, and visit Latin America without any issues. Also, a published author? I had no idea what this entailed when I originally wrote it down in the 90s. I even forgot that it was one of my goals. But one day, while flipping through some old planners amongst the dusty totes stored at my father's house, I saw those words. "I am a published author."

## Be specific

The power of these affirmations is so strong that you have to be careful what you ask for. When I wrote down, "I live near a body of water," I thought of a beautiful lake house, a beach house, or even a farmhouse with a pond. Then one day, as I looked out the window of my Cape Girardeau, Missouri studio apartment, I saw it and thought, *shit*. There it was, the mighty and ugly, Mississippi River— a body of water.

Another one of my requests was for an unexpected $10,000. The affirmation was to the effect, "I receive $10,000 unexpectedly in the mail." Well, I did. I got a check for $10,000 in the mail. However, it was a loan from my retirement account. I didn't know it when I took that loan out for no reason, but I was making my affirmation come true. When it finally hit me, I again thought to myself, *shit*.

I now ask for my unexpected money to come free and clear and to live near an ocean or a lake. I might have to add a "river or stream that bares wild trout" because that will also be acceptable.

## The perfect journal

I always knew my nightly journaling routine was missing something, but there weren't enough lines in my little notepad to accommodate my affirmations along with everything else.

I kept my bulky affirmations book separate from my journal. When I was living in my van, I stored it somewhere out of the way and forgot about it—neglecting my goals for quite some time. Now that I am creating the perfect journal, I have added room for five daily affirmations giving myself, and you, the power to create the life we want.

## Upgrade your affirmations.

I have always known to write affirmations in the first person present tense. "I am a published author," for example. What I have learned in recent years is to take it to another level by adding a gerund (ing form of the verb) to your statement. From what I understand, the key is to see yourself do(ing) the task. Not having done it, but currently doing it.

So, "I am a published author" would turn into something like, "I am publishing two books a year." or, "I am publishing my first novel."

## Here are some more examples:

"I bench-press 300 pounds" can turn into "I am bench-pressing 300 pounds," or you can get even more detailed and specific, "I am easily bench-pressing 300 pounds for ten reps." What if you only get two? Who cares?

"I run a marathon," would be, "I am running a marathon," or "I am crossing the finish line of my first marathon."

Feel free to use different verbs like "loving" or "enjoying."

"I weigh 225 pounds," can turn into, "I am enjoying life living at my goal weight of 225 pounds."

"I am debt-free," could be, "I am enjoying my debt-free life."

## Still think this is a little kooky?

Let me tell you something, if you ever held your tongue because you thought you might jinx something, asked for prayers to help someone or something, meditated on a matter, or "put it out to the universe," then you believe in the power of words. Why not use those words to get what you want out of life?

Also, if you believe that we were created in "His" image, then you should know we have the power to be creators.


## How to do it.

Every night write down five affirmations. I suggest you keep a few from the night before until you accomplish them then replace them with another. Feel free to drop an affirmation if you simply change your mind or want help manifesting something else. Please do not waste your energy creating something you no longer want. Also, when you write these, I'd say at least two should be from your "six months to live" to-do list. (Which, I get into next.)

# Six months to live

"A doctor gave a man six months to live. The man couldn't pay his bill, so he gave him another six months."
~ Henny Youngman

I have an exercise I started doing in 2014 that is not a part of my journaling, but I feel that it is so effective that I need to share it with you here.

The exercise is quite simple; write down five things for your bucket list. Easy, right? We all have our bucket lists. Maybe we haven't written it down, but we post them on Facebook. A hotel made of ice in Iceland? Oh hell yeah, bucket list! Photo op at Machu Picchu? Bucket list! Zip-line through the canopy in Costa Rica? You know it, bucket list.

I have news for you; these are wishful dreams that most will never achieve. However, you can turn your bucket list into an eye-opening and life-changing tool with just one change. Put a deadline on it.

Write out a to-do list imagining you only had six months to live. Boom, that's it. You now have a list that consists of your most important priorities in life.

One of the best benefits of this exercise is that it allows you to see what your priorities are.

I bet spending the night in an Ice Hotel won't be on this list. The trip, the car, the watch, none of these things you thought you wanted will make that list. However, it's totally cool if anything like this does make your list. (Now that I think about it, I would take my wife back to Venice, Italy and take her on the gondola ride I was too cheap to take her on many years ago.) It's just very unlikely that the things you thought you wanted are still what comes to mind when you realize you only have six months to live.

Whatever you do write down will be your priority. It will separate the meaningless crap from what you truly want out of life. This itself is a precious gift. It lets you know what you should be working on every day.

The other benefit is that this exercise sets things in motion. Not only have you listed your priorities in life, you just took action. You physically did something to get you toward the five most important things you want to achieve in your life. You've written them down.

## So let it be written, so let it be done.

I can't express enough the importance of writing things down. It is the whole point of this journal. I have found writing down certain things improve my life. This journal is a place for me to put them all. A place to give thanks, show my accomplishments, unload the stuff I have to do, and create the things I want. When I do this daily, I get everything in life I want.

Back in 2016, I stumbled across a picture of my first "Six Months to Live" to-do list. It literally was a picture of the handwritten list I made. I had forgotten about it, but because I often scroll through my photos looking for one to use in an essay or article, I saw it. Much to my surprise, in less than two years, I had achieved everything on that list.

**2014 Six-months to live list:**

Buy a van
Travel the U.S.
Take pictures
Love, love, love
Get a dog

Not only had I prioritized the most important things in my life, but in just two years, I achieved them all. Again, this is the power of writing things down. After realizing that I accomplished everything on this list, I thought why not write out another one and see what happens.

**Below is the updated six months to live list from 2016 with some 2019 commentary:**

Have Sex! I was quite celibate when I originally made this list. Needless to say, I have a son so…
Write two manuscripts. I think I wrote more than two.
Get an accurate diagnosis. I was referring to the hell I went through for a couple of years with the VA. I am happy to say that I have since been diagnosed with depression and put on some life-changing medications.
See more of my country. I was referring to being in my second year of life on the road and not having traveled to any new states. I did make it to Wyoming for about 24 hours, but that was it. I saw a lot more of Colorado that I had never seen before. So, that kind of counts.

Just like I did when I came across my list from 2014, once I saw that I had achieved everything on my 2016 list, I decided to write a new (2019) list.

Get life insurance. Just because I only have six months to live doesn't mean my insurance company needs to know that. My life is changing. I have others to think about now.

Write and publish three books. I need to finish the last book of my series about Pierre Bernal de los Campos. I have the first draft of my childhood memoir written. I need to publish it. I would like to write a book for my son—a magical folklore tale of his great grandmother.

Take lots of pictures. Everything so far seems to focus around leaving a legacy for my son. This would include photos. I have a love for photography and would literally take pictures until the day I die. Also, I think he'd love to see pictures his father took. I hope that it would inspire him to be creative in any medium he desired.

Marry *You Know Who*. My son's mother should have the same last name as him. Also, marrying *You Know Who* is the one thing I have wanted to do the most since we first dated in 2003.

Move to Colorado. I want to live in the mountains, fly fish, and build fires every day until I die. *You Know Who* can move back to Missouri after I'm dead.

As of right now, I got some decent insurance through work. I already published one book. This one in your hand will be the second. Plus, I have a rough draft written about my son's great-grandmother. Now that I have a son, I take quite a bit of pictures. If you follow me on Instagram (@davidesotojr), you already know this. I married *You Know Who* in March 2019. And as far a moving to Colorado, that one could take a while.

I updated the above "six months to live" to-do list in February of 2019. Do you want to guess when I am writing this? It's June 2019. It has been five months, and I have already achieved four out of the five things on my list. Again, this is the power of writing things down.

## Not thinking about it doesn't mean it won't happen.

I originally posted this exercise on Tumblr back in 2014, challenging my followers to write out their own list. Someone commented that she found it depressing to think about dying in six months and that she would just eat whatever she wanted. If that's you, write it down. I bet seeing that Twinkies were one of your priorities in life would be an eye-opener.

That very woman ended up making her list and shared it with me. I don't remember everything on it, but I do remember one of them was "Plan My Wedding." All I could think to say to her was "What the eff are you waiting for? If this is the first thing you would do if you knew you were going to die, what could be more important?" I didn't, though. I just hoped that she could now see what her priorities were. I can't imagine anything stopping me from marrying the person I love. What could be more important? I wonder if she's married now.

I keep mentioning that this journal is for me. I want to have a place to write down my lists and reference it as often as I want. When I wrote my first list down, I happened to take a picture of it for a blog post. If I hadn't done this, I wouldn't have had a record of it. I wouldn't have been able to see it two years later and realize that I had accomplished everything on it.

As far as the two following lists, I never did write them down except for in the blog post I wrote. I had to find that essay to look at my list. This is why I am providing the space below:

_____

_____

_____

_____

_____

_____

_____

_____

_____

_____

_____

_____

_____

_____

# Journal

# How You See Yourself

"You can not consistently perform in a manner that is inconsistent with the way you see yourself." ~Zig Ziglar

When I had my own company, I paid myself a salary based on $14 an hour at 40 hours a week. When I lost that company, I started looking for work based on what I paid myself.

Jobs paying $14, $15, or even $17 an hour were easy to come by. The problem was it required I actually work 40 hours a week. That did not seem very appealing.

Then it hit me. *Why am I looking for a $14-$19 an hour job?*

I am a retired Master Sergeant. I have been in the building trades since I was 18 years old. I have been to war. I got my first job as a supervisor at the age of 24. I became the head of the HVAC department for a trade school at 28. Most of all, I was the President and CEO of a company I started from nothing.

I was a leader, a manager, and everything else that came with the title Founder, CEO, and President. I just hadn't seen myself as such.

Once I did, I started applying for positions that paid what I was worth. Eventually, I landed a job with a salary that was more than twice what I earned as the CEO of my own company. All I did differently was change the way I saw myself.

**Date** _____

## Accomplishments

1) _____
2) _____
3) _____
4) _____
5) _____

## Gratitude

1) _____
2) _____
3) _____
4) _____
5) _____

## Affirmations

1) _____
2) _____
3) _____
4) _____
5) _____

## Tomorrow

1) _____
2) _____
3) _____
4) _____
5) _____

# Humility

"When pride cometh, then cometh shame: but with the lowly is wisdom." ~Proverbs 11:2

The word for low in Latin is humilis. Humilis is the word origin for humility and humble. So it makes sense that later translations of the Bible replaced the words "the lowly" with "humility."

To err is human. It's how we learn—how we progress in life.

On my first trip to Guanajuato, Mexico, a couple of roommates and I went on a trek to the city of León, a city known for its leather goods. I had seen a friend come back from there with a cool messenger bag and I wanted one just like it.

Somewhere in the city, we got lost or confused. I don't exactly remember the reason why, but I know we needed directions. My male roommate and I both refused to ask. Not because we were too stubborn to ask for directions, but because we both didn't want to look dumb trying to speak Spanish. We were both fairly new to the language.

Our other roommate, however, did not care how "dumb" she looked. And even though my male roommate and I both spoke better Spanish, she took it upon herself to ask for directions.

I winced when I heard her butcher the language. She didn't roll her Rs and her vocabulary was minimal—how embarrassing. But because she had the humility to be flawed, we got the directions we needed.

You can apply this lesson to life. Have somewhere you want to be—a goal you want to attain? Be prepared to make some mistakes or be prepared to go nowhere.

Date _____

## Accomplishments

    1) _____

    2) _____

    3) _____

    4) _____

    5) _____

## Gratitude

    1) _____

    2) _____

    3) _____

    4) _____

    5) _____

## Affirmations

    1) _____

    2) _____

    3) _____

    4) _____

    5) _____

## Tomorrow

    1) _____

    2) _____

    3) _____

    4) _____

    5) _____

# Don't take anyone's word for it

There is a lot of information out there. Everyone has their opinions and are not afraid to post them online. One Google search will yield thousands of blogs, websites, forums, pictures, tweets, and who knows what else. How do you determine what to believe and what is nonsense?

Over the years I have developed a process that helps me decide whether to believe in something or not. I find that applying all three of the questions below works best, but individually, they are strong enough to stand on their own.

## What does your gut tell you?

Whatever your belief system is, that gut feeling is a higher power talking to you. It can be God, the Universe, or Quantum Mechanics. Who cares? This feeling in your gut is not something to disregard. Listen to it.

## Do two people you consider credible sources agree with your gut?

Do people you trust also feel the same way? They can be authors, subject matter experts, professionals, or whoever's opinion YOU respect.

## What does your personal experience tell you?

If kale makes you break out in a rash, it doesn't matter how many articles you've read or how many people tell you it is good for you. You know the truth first hand.

**Date** _____

## Accomplishments

1) _____

2) _____

3) _____

4) _____

5) _____

## Gratitude

1) _____

2) _____

3) _____

4) _____

5) _____

## Affirmations

1) _____

2) _____

3) _____

4) _____

5) _____

## Tomorrow

1) _____

2) _____

3) _____

4) _____

5) _____

# Everything has a Sweet Spot

In Malcolm Gladwell's book, *David and Goliath*, he refers to how the number of students in a classroom can affect their academic achievement. Too many students and their grades drop, too little and results are similar. To show exactly how this worked he used an illustration. That illustration was the Inverted U Curve.

## The Inverted U Curve

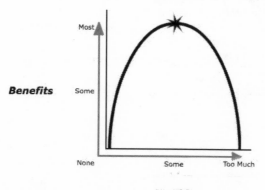

**Anything**

The Inverted U Curve is the visualization of the phrase, "Everything in Moderation."

Malcolm Gladwell had several examples of how the Inverted U Curve worked. It made me realize that it applies to everything, EVERYTHING. Good or bad, if you have too little or too much of something, the benefits will diminish.

No matter what it is, fast food, exercises, aspirin, relaxation, everything will have a sweet spot.

**Date** _____

## Accomplishments

1) _____

2) _____

3) _____

4) _____

5) _____

## Gratitude

1) _____

2) _____

3) _____

4) _____

5) _____

## Affirmations

1) _____

2) _____

3) _____

4) _____

5) _____

## Tomorrow

1) _____

2) _____

3) _____

4) _____

5) _____

## Pay Cash For Everything

If you cannot pay cash for it, you cannot afford it. Period.

Yes, I know Kevin Smith maxed out all his credit cards to finance *Clerks*, which in turn jump-started his film career. And yes he is super rich now because of it. But can you name another example of someone who has done that?

For every Kevin Smith, I bet that there are at least several thousand people who didn't make it and are now in debt.

A better example would be Quentin Tarantino who took the money he got from the sale of a script, *Natural Born Killers*, to make his breakthrough movie, *Reservoir Dogs*.

I implore you to pay cash for everything. Nothing you want is worth being in debt. There is no better feeling in the world than not owing anyone anything. That is true freedom.

**Date** _____

## Accomplishments

1) _____

2) _____

3) _____

4) _____

5) _____

## Gratitude

1) _____

2) _____

3) _____

4) _____

5) _____

## Affirmations

1) _____

2) _____

3) _____

4) _____

5) _____

## Tomorrow

1) _____

2) _____

3) _____

4) _____

5) _____

## Ask, and You Shall Receive

"Ask, and it shall be given you; seek, and ye shall find; knock, and it shall be opened unto you." Matthew 7:7

Whether you are asking the universe or praying to God, ask, and you shall receive. For years I have been writing down my goals in the form of positive affirmations, and for years I have been getting everything I asked. But be sure that you are specific when you ask. I used to say that I lived near a body of water. I was thinking of the ocean or a lake. Then one morning I woke up with a view of one of the nastiest body of water there is—the Mississippi River.

**Date** _____

## Accomplishments

1) _____

2) _____

3) _____

4) _____

5) _____

## Gratitude

1) _____

2) _____

3) _____

4) _____

5) _____

## Affirmations

1) _____

2) _____

3) _____

4) _____

5) _____

## Tomorrow

1) _____

2) _____

3) _____

4) _____

5) _____

# Creativity, Use it or Lose it

When a creative idea comes to you, act on it. If you don't, it will leave and find someone who will.

I was obsessed with film in the 1990s. I wanted to make movies like Robert Rodriguez and Quentin Tarantino.

I wasn't a writer then. Actually, I probably was. I just didn't have the self-confidence to write anything other than journal entries. I did have ideas, though—lots of them.

One idea in particular had a great ending. It's beautiful and tragic and would probably leave the audience shocked with their mouths open —popcorn kernels trapped in their teeth. I should have started writing this story then, but I didn't do a thing. That was around 1996.

In 2002, Al Udeid Air Base, Qatar, was what is known as a tent city. We worked in tents, slept in tents, and crapped in tents. Once a week a movie played at the outdoor theater, which was just several sheets of plywood pieced together and painted white. One night as I sat on a cheap, white, plastic, stackable patio chair, I watched my tragic ending unfold on the plywood movie screen. It happened just as I had imagined it. It was nearly perfect. There were a couple of things I would have done differently. I remember thinking to myself, Mother F*cker. That's my ending!

A creative idea came to me, and because I didn't act on it, it found someone else. And that guy made it into a movie with Tom Cruise.

**Date** _____

## Accomplishments

1) _____

2) _____

3) _____

4) _____

5) _____

## Gratitude

1) _____

2) _____

3) _____

4) _____

5) _____

## Affirmations

1) _____

2) _____

3) _____

4) _____

5) _____

## Tomorrow

1) _____

2) _____

3) _____

4) _____

5) _____

# Make sure your job depends on you, not the other way around.

It's perfectly fine if doing what you love doesn't pay the bills. Get a job, but don't set yourself up for misery.

People tend to base their cost of living on their income. When they realize that they hate their job, they're stuck. They can't quit because of the pay. If they were to get fired or laid off, they'd really be in trouble. This is an example of depending on your job.

Get to the point in your career that you can get out if you want to. No matter the reason—the boss is a jerk, you hate the environment, want to take the family on a summer trip to Europe—put yourself in a situation where you can walk at a moments notice.

How do you do this? The process is simple: live below your means, become debt free, save some money.

I've known dirtbags that lived on the cheap and worked somewhere like Whole Foods only long enough to save some money and hit the road again. Some of them were such hard workers that they had a job waiting for them when they came back. That's having your job depend on you.

Let's say you're a suburbanite who has a family and corporate gig paying close to six figures. The process is the same, live below your means, get out of debt, save some money. It's just spanned over years instead of months.

No, you don't have to quit your job and take a two-year long road trip, but imagine the feeling of being able to do it if you wanted to.

**Date** _____

## Accomplishments

1) _____
2) _____
3) _____
4) _____
5) _____

## Gratitude

1) _____
2) _____
3) _____
4) _____
5) _____

## Affirmations

1) _____
2) _____
3) _____
4) _____
5) _____

## Tomorrow

1) _____
2) _____
3) _____
4) _____
5) _____

## You have control over everything in your life except other people

I refused to admit that I was a controlling person. Who was I kidding? I was a control freak. I can say that now. I can look at my past behavior and see what I was doing but at the time, I had no idea.

You may not think it's controlling behavior, but if you get upset because people aren't acting or responding to a situation the way you want them to, you're upset because you don't have control. You'll never have that power over other people. If you do, know that it's manipulation, not control and that it's only temporary.

As I become older I am learning that life can be summed up in just a few phrases. The one that applies in this instance is Mind Your Own Business.

**Date** _____

## Accomplishments

1) _____

2) _____

3) _____

4) _____

5) _____

## Gratitude

1) _____

2) _____

3) _____

4) _____

5) _____

## Affirmations

1) _____

2) _____

3) _____

4) _____

5) _____

## Tomorrow

1) _____

2) _____

3) _____

4) _____

5) _____

## Winners Often Quit

Never give up but quit often.

A lot of the success and motivational material out there has to do with never giving up or quitting. You know, "Winners never quit" and such. I am coming to find out that winners do quit. They really do. And all the success stories out there are of winners who have quit.

"I have not failed. I've just found 10,000 ways that won't work." ~Thomas Edison, referencing the creation of light bulb.

For most people, this quote insinuates, "don't quit." I have to disagree. Yes, he was persistent. Yes, he did not give up, but he had to realize that certain techniques or materials were not going to work. He had to quit several times over.

**Date** _____

## Accomplishments

1) _____

2) _____

3) _____

4) _____

5) _____

## Gratitude

1) _____

2) _____

3) _____

4) _____

5) _____

## Affirmations

1) _____

2) _____

3) _____

4) _____

5) _____

## Tomorrow

1) _____

2) _____

3) _____

4) _____

5) _____

# Don't Fake It Till You Make It

This is bad advice. So many people will see that you are faking it in the process and will remember you for your dishonesty above all else.

Many years ago when I was a young HVAC instructor, I had a boss that said to never say, *I don't know*. "It will compromise your integrity with the students," he said. I remember thinking, *I don't think he knows what integrity means*. When I later needed clarification with what exactly happens with a low charge and a low evaporator temperature, I asked one of his other instructors for help. This instructor gave me an answer, and I thought, *Ok. Makes sense, I guess*. A year or two later, as I got more knowledgeable, I discovered the real answer to my question and realized that the instructor whom I asked, did not actually know the answer. He made it up.

I will always remember these men as dishonest people. Always.

**Date** _____

## Accomplishments

1) _____
2) _____
3) _____
4) _____
5) _____

## Gratitude

1) _____
2) _____
3) _____
4) _____
5) _____

## Affirmations

1) _____
2) _____
3) _____
4) _____
5) _____

## Tomorrow

1) _____
2) _____
3) _____
4) _____
5) _____

## Take the Money Out

When it comes to making decisions, take the money out of the process. There is so much more to life than money. Yeah, I know this is easy to say, especially when you have money. But I have had it and not had it and regardless, any decisions I have made based on money have never turned out well for me.

I recently turned down a job that was going to pay very well. That was the ONLY benefit. I couldn't, in good conscience, take this position knowing the negative impact it was going to have on my family in the future. Whether you are buying, hiring, or earning, base your decisions on anything else but money. I suggest love.

**Date** _____

## Accomplishments

1)_____

2) _____

3) _____

4) _____

5) _____

## Gratitude

1)_____

2) _____

3) _____

4) _____

5) _____

## Affirmations

1)_____

2) _____

3) _____

4) _____

5) _____

## Tomorrow

1)_____

2) _____

3) _____

4) _____

5) _____

## Take Care of Number 1

If you will do anything for your kids, then take care of yourself.

Now, this is one of the few things I talk about that I haven't learned from real-life experience. I have, however, been exposed to it over and over again throughout the years. I've known a lot of mothers, and I have witnessed them "sacrifice" their own health and wellbeing for the sake of their kids. This is a bad decision.

What good are you as a parent if you are dead? It seems a little dramatic, I know. But this is how serious I think people need to take this advice. You're no good as a parent dead, depressed, sick, unfulfilled, angry, or whatever else is wrong with you.

### More is caught than taught.

You are setting an example for your children. Do you really want to teach them to sacrifice their own health and happiness for someone they love—or think they love?

Whether you like it or not, your kids are going to be just like you. So get your shit together.

**Date** _____

## Accomplishments

1) _____

2) _____

3) _____

4) _____

5) _____

## Gratitude

1) _____

2) _____

3) _____

4) _____

5) _____

## Affirmations

1) _____

2) _____

3) _____

4) _____

5) _____

## Tomorrow

1) _____

2) _____

3) _____

4) _____

5) _____

## Everyone has the right to do whatever the eff they want.

I have been super-critical of people over the years. Basically, if I didn't like how they did things or the things they chose to do, I'd give them a rash of shit for it. Luckily, I have learned that people, to include myself, can do whatever the hell they want. They can eat what they want, sleep with whom they want, collect what they want, dress how they want-it's none of your business and it's none of mine. Imagine a world where everyone minded his or her own business.

Now you may think what about crimes—murder, rape, etc? Well, that's what consequences are for. Just like the outcome of eating doughnuts every day, or sleeping around unprotected, it could result in life-changing or life-threatening results. Yes, we have laws, but it is your right to break them if you want. Just know that there are consequences to pay.

As a boy on summer vacation one July, my father warned me not to light any of our leftover firecrackers while he was at work. Guess what the first thing my brother and I did that day? We knew the consequences, and we made the choice. Unfortunately for us, the next door neighbor was home sick and told on us later that evening. We paid for our bad decision.

My suggestion, relieve yourself of all the burdens that come with being concerned about what people do. Let them do whatever they want. Just don't let them do it to you if you don't want it.

Date _____

## Accomplishments

1) _____

2) _____

3) _____

4) _____

5) _____

## Gratitude

1) _____

2) _____

3) _____

4) _____

5) _____

## Affirmations

1) _____

2) _____

3) _____

4) _____

5) _____

## Tomorrow

1) _____

2) _____

3) _____

4) _____

5) _____

## Feelings are a choice

I used to not believe this. I had a friend that always told me that love is a choice. I would scoff and laugh at how ridiculous she was. I thought love was this magical thing that happened on its own—something we had no control over. Funny how it always "just happened" to me when my partners were gorgeous. I see now that it was always a choice. That means if love is a choice so are all the other emotions—like anger—something I never really wanted to take responsibility for. I claimed that this too was an instant spontaneous reaction that I had no control over. Then I learned that our emotions are a result of our thoughts. Change your thoughts and you change your feelings.

Here is an example:

Twin boys were raised by an alcoholic father. One became a drunk, the other, a success in all aspects of the word. When the drunk was asked how he got to where he was in life, he answered, "My father was an alcoholic. I was destined to be like him." When the successful man was asked how he got to where he was in life, he answered, "My father was an alcoholic. I was destined to not be like him."

One circumstance, two different thoughts, two different outcomes.

**Date** _____

## Accomplishments

1) _____

2) _____

3) _____

4) _____

5) _____

## Gratitude

1) _____

2) _____

3) _____

4) _____

5) _____

## Affirmations

1) _____

2) _____

3) _____

4) _____

5) _____

## Tomorrow

1) _____

2) _____

3) _____

4) _____

5) _____

# You are a reflection of the company you keep

"He that walketh with wise men shall be wise: but a companion of fools shall be destroyed." Proverbs 13:20

If you want to be a successful entrepreneur, you should surround yourself with successful entrepreneurs. If you want to be fit and healthy, you should not be hanging around overweight, sick people. It's that simple. The people you surround yourself with have a direct influence on who you are. This is why having a mentor is so important.

I know two of my peers who are now E-9s. This is the last stripe you can earn in the military. The highest enlisted rank there is. Though we joined the military at about the same time, I retired as an E-7 while these two will end their career at the highest enlisted rank possible. So what is the big difference between these two gentlemen and myself? Among many things, one thing they had that I did not was an E-9 for a mentor.

**Date** _____

## Accomplishments

1) _____

2) _____

3) _____

4) _____

5) _____

## Gratitude

1) _____

2) _____

3) _____

4) _____

5) _____

## Affirmations

1) _____

2) _____

3) _____

4) _____

5) _____

## Tomorrow

1) _____

2) _____

3) _____

4) _____

5) _____

# The most important conversation you can have is with yourself

I know it seems kind of silly to say nice things about yourself, especially if you have low self-esteem. But I will tell you this; it has an immense amount of power.

If you continuously tell yourself something positive, you will eventually believe it, and it will become true.

Saying something positive like, "I wear a size 34 pants," even if it's not true. (Let's say you wear a 40.) In due time you will fit into some 34s. What if I'm wrong and you get down to a 36? Still not bad, right?

Let's assume you gave it a shot—a sort of experiment and found that you now have a job promotion, or a finished manuscript, or a better relationship, or are no longer sick. Would you then see the power in positive self-talk? Now, wouldn't the opposite also be true?

## Stop the negative self-talk.

I have witnessed numerous people close to me say things about themselves that I would consider an insult had anyone else said it.

You wouldn't let anyone bully your child or your little sister. Why would you let anyone bully you? Especially you.

**Date** _____

## Accomplishments

1) _____

2) _____

3) _____

4) _____

5) _____

## Gratitude

1) _____

2) _____

3) _____

4) _____

5) _____

## Affirmations

1) _____

2) _____

3) _____

4) _____

5) _____

## Tomorrow

1) _____

2) _____

3) _____

4) _____

5) _____

# Find something you love to do and do it

People who spend time doing what they love become better people overall and as a result, become better husbands, wives, parents, bosses, employees, brothers, cousins, whatever. I think when you do what you love, everything in your life will improve, thus making your life better overall.

And no it doesn't have to be your job. Isn't that a relief? Go to work at Whole Foods or something. Get that health insurance. Just wake up an hour early and play those video games, write that manuscript, cook the kids breakfast, go to Crossfit. Whatever it is you love to do, do it.

## Do what you love and the money will follow?

Mmm maybe, but that doesn't mean you'll get paid for it. It means that you'll be such a happier person overall that whatever you do to make money, you'll be better at. You'll get more clients, a promotion, a bonus; who knows?

Just think about it; who would you rather spend time with—someone who has this unsatisfied deep down desire to do something but can't or the person who feels joy because they practice the gift that God has given them?

**Date** _____

## Accomplishments

1) _____
2) _____
3) _____
4) _____
5) _____

## Gratitude

1) _____
2) _____
3) _____
4) _____
5) _____

## Affirmations

1) _____
2) _____
3) _____
4) _____
5) _____

## Tomorrow

1) _____
2) _____
3) _____
4) _____
5) _____

# Money doesn't bring happiness, it accentuates it

This is good, right? Makes sense. The problem is, money is not prejudiced and will accentuate everything. Happiness, love, excitement for life as well as depression, anger, and all around douchebaggery. You don't think that jerk in the Audi became a jerk when he started earning six figures, do you? He always was a jerk and now that he has money he is even more of one.

Money gives you the power to reinforce your habits and behavior. It will not pull you out of a deep depression. It will plunge you deeper into it. Think of all the celebrities who have committed suicide. Why would someone with that much success do such a thing? Because they were depressed before they had money.

There is nothing wrong with wanting to be rich but don't think it has the power to make your life better. You have that power with or without money.

**Date** _____

## Accomplishments

1)_____

2) _____

3) _____

4) _____

5) _____

## Gratitude

1)_____

2) _____

3) _____

4) _____

5) _____

## Affirmations

1)_____

2) _____

3) _____

4) _____

5) _____

## Tomorrow

1)_____

2) _____

3) _____

4) _____

5) _____

# Money comes from hard work—period

When I first heard the term passive income, I knew that was for me. I wanted money just to come in while I do nothing. It sounded like the perfect scenario. I began learning as much on the subject as possible. I bought the books, the audiotapes, and the tickets to the seminars. It seemed peculiar that I made a living by working and then sent money to those people who were teaching me about how to have passive income, but I stayed the course.

It took me years and thousands of dollars to figure out that there is no such thing. Even these fools who swear up and down that passive income is a thing, work their butts off selling this garbage. If they didn't their income would disappear.

Can you make money while you sleep? Yes. But it requires lots of work.

Whether you turn wrenches, dig ditches, or sell intellectual property online, money won't come unless you work for it. That's it.

**Date** _____

## Accomplishments

1) _____

2) _____

3) _____

4) _____

5) _____

## Gratitude

1) _____

2) _____

3) _____

4) _____

5) _____

## Affirmations

1) _____

2) _____

3) _____

4) _____

5) _____

## Tomorrow

1) _____

2) _____

3) _____

4) _____

5) _____

# Success is the ability to do what you love

I have been trying to figure out the definition of success for a while. I've made videos, Instagram posts, and tweets asking people what their definition of success is. Crickets! Nobody seems to want to answer this question. Or could it be that they don't know the answer? Does anyone know the answer? One would think that with all the "success" coaches, speakers, courses, books, and whatever else out there, someone would know what success is.

Then one day I heard Vagabonding author Rolf Potts say this, "The definition of success is being able to do what you want whenever you want to do it." I thought, *That's it. That is the definition of success.*

This definition allows you to define success however you want. It could be anything—travel, raising a family, buying a car, living in Spain. This definition of success applies to everyone, not just those who want to be rich. As perfect as I thought it was, something didn't settle with me. I continued to ask people how they defined success. I am not sure why, though. Hadn't I found the perfect answer?

Then one night while lying in bed, just moments away from falling asleep I discovered my own definition.

"Success is the ability to do what you love."

If you are doing what you love, whether it's part time, full time, or as a hobby, you are a success.

**Date** _____

## Accomplishments

   1)_____

   2) _____

   3) _____

   4) _____

   5) _____

## Gratitude

   1)_____

   2) _____

   3) _____

   4) _____

   5) _____

## Affirmations

   1)_____

   2) _____

   3) _____

   4) _____

   5) _____

## Tomorrow

   1)_____

   2) _____

   3) _____

   4) _____

   5) _____

# Do no harm—especially to yourself

Live like you were dying. Blah blah blah. I know I like to say that this is how we should live our life, but is this sustainable? Is this a realistic way of thinking? Wouldn't we just indulge in our vices if this were how we were supposed to live our lives? Probably. But I think this is where we need to apply one of the very few rules of life: Do no harm.

Do whatever you want, just not at the expense of others. It's that simple. Keep in mind that the most important person you should not harm is yourself.

**Date** _____

## Accomplishments

1) _____

2) _____

3) _____

4) _____

5) _____

## Gratitude

1) _____

2) _____

3) _____

4) _____

5) _____

## Affirmations

1) _____

2) _____

3) _____

4) _____

5) _____

## Tomorrow

1) _____

2) _____

3) _____

4) _____

5) _____

## Let something that no one can take away from you be what brings you happiness

When I discovered fly-fishing, I found something that brought me joy—something so peaceful, so simple, so satisfying. Living in Colorado, I was able to incorporate fishing into my life nearly every day. Then, the love of my life reached out to me, and just like that, I move back to St. Louis. If fly-fishing were my source of happiness, I would have left my happiness in the Rocky Mountains.

Things, events, places, and people can bring you joy but when it comes to happiness, it has to come from within or somebody can take it away from you.

And somebody includes God. I have seen the death of a loved one ruin someone's life.

**Date** _____

## Accomplishments

1) _____

2) _____

3) _____

4) _____

5) _____

## Gratitude

1) _____

2) _____

3) _____

4) _____

5) _____

## Affirmations

1) _____

2) _____

3) _____

4) _____

5) _____

## Tomorrow

1) _____

2) _____

3) _____

4) _____

5) _____

# People will treat you as poorly as you allow them

Stop allowing people to treat you like crap. This might be easier said than done but I know it's possible as I have been the one who treated people like crap.

I once dropped some suggestive hints to a former lover completely disregarding the fact that she was in a committed relationship.

"You are not allowed to talk to me that way anymore," she said.

My response? "Ok." And that was it.

In actuality, she was a pretty good friend and I wanted to maintain a relationship with her as she did with me. But now there was going to have to be mutual respect for one another. I agreed, right then and there on the phone.

Then there was a time I got into an argument with a coworker and I started to raise my voice. She very calmly said to me, "Please don't yell at me."

"Oh, sorry," I said and continued our conversation without yelling.

In the former example, my friend drew the line after years of torment. In the latter, she drew it right off the bat. In both cases, out of respect for them I easily complied with their request.

What if I hadn't? Then they would have walked. In both cases, these women had enough self-respect that they would not carry on a relationship of any kind with someone who treated them poorly.

**Date** _____

## Accomplishments

1) _____
2) _____
3) _____
4) _____
5) _____

## Gratitude

1) _____
2) _____
3) _____
4) _____
5) _____

## Affirmations

1) _____
2) _____
3) _____
4) _____
5) _____

## Tomorrow

1) _____
2) _____
3) _____
4) _____
5) _____

## You can't do it on your own

Maybe you can. But why would you if you could get it done ten, twenty, or a hundred times faster, especially if you don't enjoy the process. I could hire someone to help me write a book, but I love the process. I am not in a hurry.

I often talk about how I have never not been able to fix an air-conditioner. If it heats or cools, I can fix it. Part of the reason for this is I always asked for help. When a church has a mass in a few hours or an Airborne Warning And Control System plane has to take off, I don't have time for pride or stubbornness. The A/C needs to be fixed as soon as possible by any means necessary. That *means* is usually help.

If you have ever uttered the words or even thought, "I can do it myself," ask yourself why. Is it because you love the process? If the answer is no, get some help.

**Date** _____

## Accomplishments

1) _____

2) _____

3) _____

4) _____

5) _____

## Gratitude

1) _____

2) _____

3) _____

4) _____

5) _____

## Affirmations

1) _____

2) _____

3) _____

4) _____

5) _____

## Tomorrow

1) _____

2) _____

3) _____

4) _____

5) _____

# Give up on retirement

This is right up there with passive income. It's a farce. Why have we been taught to strive for this for our entire lives? Why should we waste the prime of our lives slaving away with hopes that one day, around the age of 65, we can THEN start to enjoy life?

After a five-month trip to Mexico one year, people started asking me if I was retired. I wasn't, but I had decided to live like I was in short spurts. Five months here, one month there. And what did I do in-between? Work.

Work allowed me to do whatever I wanted. Work fed me and paid the bills. Work padded my savings account. Work provided me with a sense of satisfaction. Why would I ever give that up?

I believe that once a person stops working, they are on their way to the grave.

But what if you hate your job. Then you have the wrong job. Give it thirty years though to see if it grows on you.

"The goal is not to STOP working; the goal is to not HAVE to work."

If you have managed to dedicate most of your adult life to a career, congratulations, now get to work doing something you love. Now is not the time to slow down. You have work to do—work you enjoy.

**Date** _____

## Accomplishments

1) _____

2) _____

3) _____

4) _____

5) _____

## Gratitude

1) _____

2) _____

3) _____

4) _____

5) _____

## Affirmations

1) _____

2) _____

3) _____

4) _____

5) _____

## Tomorrow

1) _____

2) _____

3) _____

4) _____

5) _____

# What other people think of you is none of your business

Remember that you have no control over other people—not their emotions, not their thoughts. So why would you care what they think of you? Let me repeat this. YOU HAVE NO CONTROL OVER WHAT OTHER PEOPLE THINK. They have all the power, which essentially makes their thoughts none of your business.

The people who love you will love you no matter what. The people who don't like you will not like you no matter what. You can't influence them either way. So stop worrying about what others think. It has nothing to do with you, and it's a waste of your energy.

**Date** _____

## Accomplishments

1) _____
2) _____
3) _____
4) _____
5) _____

## Gratitude

1) _____
2) _____
3) _____
4) _____
5) _____

## Affirmations

1) _____
2) _____
3) _____
4) _____
5) _____

## Tomorrow

1) _____
2) _____
3) _____
4) _____
5) _____

# Get out of debt

"The rich ruleth over the poor, and the borrower is servant to the lender." Proverbs 22:7

If you are in debt, you are a slave. Don't believe me; try not working for a while. You can't. You don't have that *freedom*.

I realized debt equated to slavery when I was forced to take a job overseas one year. My personal training company had gone under, and I did not have the money to pay my bills. Because I had debt, I had to work. After a few months at this horrible job, I couldn't take it anymore and wanted to quit but I couldn't. I had a house payment, a car payment, and $20,000 in credit card debt. Not working was not an option. I sucked it up and pushed through the misery. When my debts were paid off, I quit. I came home with nothing, but I was free, no longer my lender's servant.

**Date** _____

## Accomplishments

1) _____

2) _____

3) _____

4) _____

5) _____

## Gratitude

1) _____

2) _____

3) _____

4) _____

5) _____

## Affirmations

1) _____

2) _____

3) _____

4) _____

5) _____

## Tomorrow

1) _____

2) _____

3) _____

4) _____

5) _____

## Learn the fundamentals so that you can concentrate on creativity

When I was an HVAC instructor, I taught electrical fundamentals in the morning and refrigeration fundamentals at night. The classes were ten weeks long. After every session, the classes swapped and I'd start again. I did this over and over again for four years.

When I eventually ended up back out in the field, I found that I was a superstar HVAC tech. I was good before, but after drilling the fundamentals in my head over and over for four years, I became great.

When you don't have to think about the basics, your mind is free to concentrate on creativity. And your creativity sets you above the rest. It's what makes your performance unique. It is your gift.

You cannot fully utilize your gift if you are too busy thinking, what is the finger position for a B-Minor chord, or how do I dribble a basketball between my legs, or should I downshift coming into this turn, or in my case, what direction is the refrigerant flowing, or what is the voltage going to this compressor supposed to be.

Before you can fully shine at a task, you have to have the fundamentals engraved in your subconscious—freeing up your conscious mind to focus on your creativity.

**Date** _____

## Accomplishments

1) _____
2) _____
3) _____
4) _____
5) _____

## Gratitude

1) _____
2) _____
3) _____
4) _____
5) _____

## Affirmations

1) _____
2) _____
3) _____
4) _____
5) _____

## Tomorrow

1) _____
2) _____
3) _____
4) _____
5) _____

# Lead by example

You are a leader, whether you know it or not. Someone out there looks up to you. Someone out there is following your lead. And if you are a parent, that someone is your child.

More is caught than taught. The first time I heard these words was from Dave Ramsey's daughter Rachael Cruze. Dave and his daughter are financial gurus. Rachael leans more toward family and children. When she said more is caught than taught, she referred to when parents are good with money (saving and investing) then so are their children. Regardless of what you teach them, you are going to set the example they are going to follow.

The more I thought about it, the more I realized "more is caught than taught" is not only restricted to finance. It could be anything—smoking, reading, or eating healthy. Whatever you want your children to do, you have to show them by doing it yourself.

Then I realized this is not restricted to one's children. This is leadership. The greatest thing you can do to lead people is set the example.

Whether you think you are in a leadership role are not, people are following your example. I have been shocked many times in my life when I have learned that there was a young man out there following my lead without me knowing. It gave me a little sense of pride—wow someone looks up to me—but it also left me with some regret. I wished I had been setting a better example.

**Date** _____

**Accomplishments**

1) _____

2) _____

3) _____

4) _____

5) _____

**Gratitude**

1) _____

2) _____

3) _____

4) _____

5) _____

**Affirmations**

1) _____

2) _____

3) _____

4) _____

5) _____

**Tomorrow**

1) _____

2) _____

3) _____

4) _____

5) _____

# Perfection guarantees failure

"If you look for perfection, you'll never be content."
~Leo Tolstoy

Do you have any examples of something that went or ended up perfect? If you do, I'd say it was not of your doing. It was circumstantial or luck like *The Perfect Storm*.

I'd say my son is perfection, but the truth is he has and misshapen head and Pectus Excavatum (sunken chest). If that is the worst my beautiful baby is going to suffer from, I am grateful. God has truly blessed me.

If you want perfection, learn to accept the imperfect.

The subtitle of this book says there are 30 days of tips and prompts when there are actually 31. I decided to add a couple more pages so that I could get the book to over a total count of 100. Imperfect? Yes, but I published it anyway. Had I not done so, it wouldn't be in your hands right now. I wouldn't have sold as many copies as I have by now. I wouldn't have made a positive impact on both our lives. It seems like a lot to lose out on because I wanted to wait until it was perfect before I published it.

Perfection does not exist, so if you are striving for it, you are in for a rude awakening—if you ever do awaken. There is a chance you never realize this and spend the rest of your life in misery because you tried to achieve the impossible.

**Date** _____

## Accomplishments

1)_____

2) _____

3) _____

4) _____

5) _____

## Gratitude

1)_____

2) _____

3) _____

4) _____

5) _____

## Affirmations

1)_____

2) _____

3) _____

4) _____

5) _____

## Tomorrow

1)_____

2) _____

3) _____

4) _____

5) _____

# What Now?

Congratulations! You worked on you for a month. Now what? Well, don't stop. While you may have noticed some positive changes in your life, it's obvious that everything can't be "fixed" in just one month. If you haven't ordered another copy of this journal, then go ahead and get on that first. This is not a practice that you can do for a while, reap the benefits, and be done. This journal is like eating healthy and exercising, it something that needs to be done every day for as long as you live.

Again, I'm not trying to dupe you into buying more of my journals. You can write these things down on a scratch piece of paper for all I care. I am trying to reinforce that this needs to be a continuous daily practice. I'll give you two good reasons why:

-Just like daily exercise and healthy eating, when you stop journaling, you'll start to feel kind of blah. You can take a day off here or there, but if you give it up completely, you'll notice the results of all your hard work start to disappear. You'll look back and wish you had never stopped and then regret that you have to start all over again.

-You'll evolve and change, and so will your desires. You may change your mind about a particular goal. Or, you may have achieved it and replaced it with another. If this journal helped you achieve your old goals, then they'll help you achieve your new ones.

You are always going to want to be better at whatever stage of life you are in.

## What about redundancy?

Do I need a journal that has daily readings that I have already read? The answer is yes. I'll tell you why.

Why do you know the lyrics to your favorite song? Repetition. Why do you know when to step on the brake and when to step on the gas when driving? Repetition. How do you know guitar chords, dance moves, test answers, etc.? Repetition. The little life lessons included in this book, need to be read over and over again to get the full benefit from them.

Does anyone ever retain every bit of information they read? I know I don't. I sometimes find that I am going to have to reread something before I am even done reading it the first time.

Have you ever watched a movie for a second or third time and catch something you missed? The same will happen when you read this material over again.

When the student is ready, the teacher will appear. In other words, depending on where you are in your life, what you read may have a different impact on you. Meanings may change, or you may not fully comprehend something because it doesn't pertain to you in that stage of your life.

I listened to and read Zig Ziglar's material for twenty years before I heard him say, "You praise in public and critique in private." The first time I heard this was not the first time I heard this. It wasn't from a new speech he had given, a new book, or a new audio recording. It came from the same material I had heard repeatedly for decades. I just wasn't ready for it until that very moment.

Rereading the material on the left side of this journal is not a waste. That is precisely what it is there for; to reread—to remind you (and me) over and over again. However, I have started working on a JBB Journal Volume II, which may or may not be published yet by the time you read this, just in case you want some variety.

# About the Author

David is a retired U.S. Air Force Master Sergeant who didn't realize until reaching his forties that he was a writer. As a child, he struggled with learning disabilities, which yielded him grades that barely earned him his high school diploma. With marks like that, the thought of being an author never occurred to him, and college was not an option. He joined the military going in and out of active duty for 23 years. The same week David took off the uniform for the last time, never to put it back on, he hit the road traveling the U.S. Southwest in his van.

David penned several health and wellness articles and books, but after listening to *On Writing* by Stephen King, he decided to give writing fiction a try. He started with a novel about an Air Force Sergeant whose PTSD caused him to do terrible things in his sleep. This project was for practice as well as fun, and he published a chapter every week on his website www.DavidSotoWrites.com. After several months, this project came to an abrupt halt.

One of Stephen King's pieces of advice was to become a voracious reader of fiction. David became obsessed with reading novels and became reacquainted with his favorite "genre," magical realism. One evening while reading, he envisioned a beautiful woman who sold magical chocolates to people who needed to rekindle the fire in their love life. That was the birth of *Los Chocolates de Esperanza Diamanté* and the series of books that followed.

Currently, David's life on the road is over, and he has settled back in St. Louis with his wife and son.

Made in the USA
Middletown, DE
18 August 2022

71621730R00064